Fact Finders®

T0080570

Asteroids, Comets, and Meteoroids

by Steve Kortenkamp

Consultant:
Dr. Ilia I. Roussev
Associate Astronomer
Institute for Astronomy
University of Hawaii at Manoa

CAPSTONE PRESS
a capstone imprint

Fact Finders are published by Capstone Press,
1710 Roe Crest Drive, North Mankato, Minnesota 56003
www.capstonepub.com

Books published by Capstone Press are manufactured with paper
containing at least 10 percent post-consumer waste.

Library of Congress Cataloging-in-Publication Data
Kortenkamp, Steve.
Asteroids, comets, and meteoroids / by Steve Kortenkamp.
 p. cm.—(Fact finders. The solar system and beyond)
 Includes bibliographical references and index.
 Summary: "Describes asteroids, comets, and meteoroids, including what they are and how scientists
research them"—Provided by publisher.
ISBN 978-1-4296-6494-3 (library binding)
ISBN 978-1-4296-7223-8 (paperback)
 1. Asteroids—Juvenile literature. 2. Comets—Juvenile literature. 3. Meteoroids—Juvenile literature.
I. Title. II. Series.
QB651.K666 2012
523.5—dc22   2011002115

Editorial Credits
Jennifer Besel, editor; Heidi Thompson, designer; Eric Manske, production specialist

Photo Credits
E. Kolmhofer, H. Raab, Johannes-Kepler-Observatory, 16; Halley Multicolor Camera Team, Giotto
Project, ESA, 26; iStockphoto: tpuezer, cover, 1; NASA, 24, 29, Ben Zellner (Georgia Southern
University), Peter Thomas (Cornell University), 11, JPL, 25, JPL/JHUAPL, 8, JPL/Keck Observatory
by C. Dumas, 10, JPL-Caltech/T. Pyle (SSC), 3, 5, JSC, 5, Tunc Tezel, 21; Photo by Michael Lipschutz,
5; Photo Researchers, Inc: Detlev van Ravenswaay, 7, 9, Science Source, 27; Photodisc, 18; Shutterstock:
Pichugin Dmitry, 23, Walter G Arce, 13

Artistic Effects
iStockphoto: Dar Yang Yan, Nickilford

Printed in the United States of America in North Mankato, Minnesota.
052017   010540R

Table of Contents

Chapter 1

Space Rocks

It was the summer of 1991 in Noblesville, Indiana. Nine-year-old Brian Kinzie and 13-year-old Brodie Spaulding were riding bikes. The boys stopped to talk. Suddenly they heard a whistling sound. Then Brian saw a black rock flying through the air. It hit the ground right behind Brodie. When the boys picked up the fist-sized rock, they discovered it was warm. This was no ordinary rock. It was a rock from space!

Planets, moons, and stars aren't the only things in space. Billions of asteroids and comets **orbit** the Sun in our solar system. Pieces that have broken off asteroids and comets float around too. All these space rocks date back to when our solar system formed.

orbit: the path an object follows as it goes around a star, planet, or asteroid

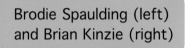
Brodie Spaulding (left)
and Brian Kinzie (right)

Noblesville meteorite

Formation of the Solar System

Four and a half billion years ago our solar system didn't exist. But there was a huge **molecular cloud**. When a nearby star exploded, the cloud collapsed in on itself. Most of the gas and dust collected in the center of the cloud. When the temperature inside the cloud reached millions of degrees, the gas started to burn. It became our Sun.

Some of the gas and dust in the molecular cloud fell into a flat disk around the Sun. Dust in the disk began sticking together and grew into rocks. Then the rocks clumped together, forming boulders. Soon round objects grew from the colliding boulders. The disk was building the rocky inner planets. The rocks that didn't form planets are what we call asteroids.

molecular cloud: a giant cloud made mostly of hydrogen atoms bound together

Farther from the Sun the disk was cold. It was so cold that some of the gas froze into ice. The ice mixed with rocks. This icy material allowed giant outer planets to form. Comets in our solar system are the icy objects leftover from the growth of the outer planets.

illustration of the solar system's formation

Chapter 2

Asteroids

Most asteroids orbit the Sun between Mars and Jupiter. This part of the solar system is called the main asteroid belt. The smallest asteroids seen in the main belt are about as wide as a soccer field. The largest main belt asteroids are hundreds of miles across.

Millions of asteroids move on different orbits in the main belt. Sometimes asteroids smash into each other. They collide at more than 5,000 miles (8,000 kilometers) per hour. These crashes form huge **craters** on the surfaces of asteroids.

up close image of asteroid Eros

crater: a hole made when large pieces of rock crash into the surface of a space object

Mars

asteroid belt

Jupiter

The Biggest Asteroids

Two of the biggest asteroids in the main belt are Ceres and Vesta. Ceres is the largest at about 600 miles (1,000 km) across. Pictures taken with the Hubble Space Telescope show that Ceres is the only round asteroid. That round shape means Ceres is also a dwarf planet. The best pictures of Ceres show that its surface is made of grayish-brown dust. The dust may cover a layer of ice. Some scientists think Ceres has an ocean of liquid water under its frozen, dusty surface.

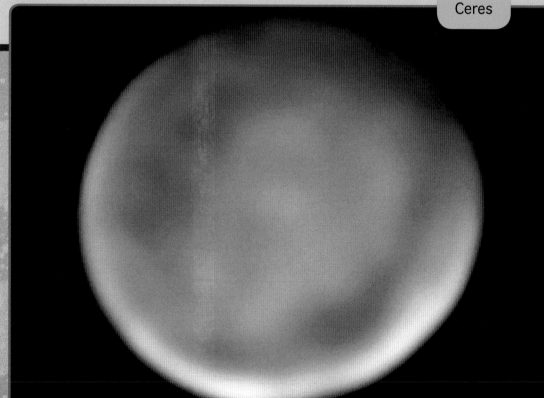

Ceres

a computer
model of Vesta

Vesta is about half the size of Ceres. It's not round, so it is not a dwarf planet. Vesta's surface reflects more sunlight than any other asteroid. This reflection makes Vesta the brightest asteroid. Vesta is so bright that sometimes it can be seen from Earth without a telescope.

Vesta has a rocky layer surrounding an iron core. It has a huge crater at its south pole. This hole in Vesta lets scientists see inside the asteroid.

Near-Earth Asteroids

Jupiter's strong **gravity** can change the orbits of some main belt asteroids. Over millions of years, Jupiter's gravity stretches the asteroids' orbits. This stretching causes the asteroids to move into the region near Earth. Scientists know of about 5,000 near-Earth asteroids. Some of them could someday hit our planet.

Many near-Earth asteroids have hit Earth. In 2008 scientists discovered a near-Earth asteroid just two days before it hit our planet. That asteroid was only about the size of a school desk. It broke apart in the **atmosphere**. The pieces landed in Africa. About 50,000 years ago an asteroid hit near what is now Flagstaff, Arizona. It exploded when it hit the ground. It made a crater that is about half a mile (.8 km) across. About 65 million years ago, the impact of an asteroid may have helped cause the extinction of the dinosaurs.

gravity: a force that pulls object together

atmosphere: the gases that surround a planet or star

the crater near
Flagstaff, Arizona

Chapter 3

Comets

Comets start their lives beyond Neptune. Billions of icy objects orbit the Sun in this trans-Neptunian region. These objects are so far from the Sun that their surface temperatures are minus 400 degrees Fahrenheit (minus 240 degrees Celsius) or colder. The objects are frozen chunks of ice, dust, and rock that scientists call "dirty snowballs."

Trans-Neptunian objects take hundreds of years to orbit the Sun. One object, named Sedna, takes about 10,500 years to go around once. Sometimes a trans-Neptunian object gets too close to Neptune. Then the giant planet's gravity stretches the object's orbit. Eventually the object passes inside the orbits of Uranus, Saturn, and Jupiter. When the object gets closer to the Sun than Jupiter, the Sun heats it up. Ice on the object's surface turns to gas. The gas blows off the surface and pulls dust with it. When gas and dust start coming off the object, it becomes a comet.

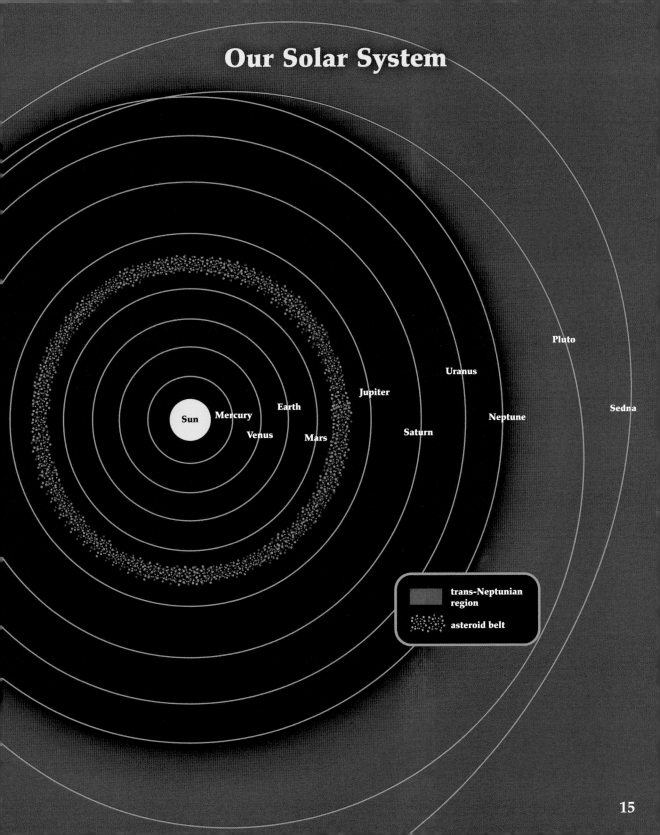

Our Solar System

Sun

Mercury

Earth

Venus

Mars

Jupiter

Saturn

Uranus

Neptune

Pluto

Sedna

trans-Neptunian region

asteroid belt

FACT: Comets grow new tails each time they get close to the Sun.

dust tail

nucleus

gas tail

coma

Parts of a Comet

Comets have several parts. The frozen "dirty snowball" part is the **nucleus**. Most comets have a nucleus about 10 miles (16 km) across. The cloud of gas and dust that comes off the nucleus as the Sun heats it is the coma. Comas surround the nucleus and are about 60,000 miles (100,000 km) across. Sunlight and **solar wind** then push the gas and dust in the coma away from the nucleus, forming long tails.

Most comets have two tails, a blue one made of gas and a white one made of dust. A comet's tails always point away from the Sun. Sunlight and solar wind push the gas and dust away from the Sun. Comet tails can stretch more than 1 million miles (1.6 million km) away from the nucleus.

The last part of a comet is called the trail. Pieces of sand, pebbles, and rocks break off the comet. These pieces are too big for sunlight to push into the tail. The trails of some comets are billions of miles long.

nucleus: the lump of ice, snow, rock, and dust that moves around the Sun

solar wind: particles blowing away from the Sun at 250 to 500 miles (400 to 800 km) per second

Halley's Comet

Halley's Comet

The most famous comet is Halley's Comet. Scientists have studied this comet for more than 2,000 years. Halley's orbit stretches from the trans-Neptunian region to Mercury's orbit.

The Sun's gravity makes objects move very fast when they are nearby. But the farther objects get from the Sun, the slower they orbit. Halley's Comet swings past the inner planets in less than one year. But it takes about 75 more years to go around the rest of its orbit.

FACT: Halley's Comet will come past Earth again in the year 2062.

Chapter 4

Meteoroids, Meteors, and Meteorites

The smallest space rocks are meteoroids. These rocks are too small for scientists to see, even with the most powerful telescopes. Meteoroids range in size from as small as a grain of sand to as large as a house. They are made when asteroids and comets break apart.

Every day, meteoroids hit Earth's atmosphere. Meteoroids entering the atmosphere travel between 25,000 and 150,000 miles (40,000 to 240,000 km) per hour. They move so fast that **friction** with the air makes them burn up. A burning meteoroid is called a meteor. Some people call meteors "falling stars," but that's not right. They are really falling rocks.

Sometimes hundreds of meteors can happen on the same night. These meteor showers occur when Earth passes through a comet's trail.

friction: the force created by a moving object as it rubs against something else

FACT: Every planet with an atmosphere can have meteors.

the Orionid meteor shower on October 20, 2003

Meteorites

Sometimes a meteoroid is too big to completely burn up in Earth's atmosphere. It hits the ground and becomes known as a meteorite.

Almost all meteorites are pieces of asteroids. Just like asteroids, they are made of iron and rock. The largest meteorite found on Earth is bigger than a car and made of solid iron. It landed in Africa thousands of years ago.

Scientists collect thousands of meteorites from Antarctica. The dark rocks are easy to spot on the bright ice. Back in their laboratories, scientists cut the meteorites into pieces. Some of the **atoms** on the inside have been around since the beginning of the solar system. Scientists study these atoms to learn how long ago our solar system formed.

atom: an element in its smallest form

FACT: Each year about 30,000 small meteorites strike Earth.

The Hoba meteorite in Namibia, Africa, is the largest known meteorite on Earth.

Chapter 5

Exploring Space Rocks

Scientists use telescopes and robotic space probes to explore asteroids and comets. The *Galileo* space probe was the first to visit asteroids. It flew by an asteroid named Gaspra in 1991 and another named Ida in 1993. Since then, other probes have explored nine other asteroids.

Pictures sent back to Earth by space probes show that asteroids have uneven, crooked shapes. They are also covered in craters like Earth's Moon. The *Galileo* probe discovered that some asteroids have moons orbiting them.

illustration of *Galileo*

an image of Gaspra
taken by *Galileo*

Studying Comets

In 1986 scientists sent five space probes to study Halley's Comet. It was the first time astronomers saw a comet nucleus up close. They learned that gas and dust come off the nucleus in fast jets on the sunlit side of the comet. But as the comet rotates, these jets turn off on the dark side. When there's no sunlight warming the night side of the comet, the ice can't turn to gas.

In 1993 scientists using a telescope discovered a comet that had broken into pieces. Jupiter's strong gravity tore the comet apart. When scientists saw the comet pieces, they learned that a comet nucleus is not one solid ball. It is made up of many small pieces that are stuck together.

the nucleus of Halley's Comet

In 2003 the *Stardust* spacecraft flew through the coma of a comet. It collected some of the comet's dust using a robot arm. The spacecraft brought the dust back to Earth for scientists to study. They learned that some of the comet dust had been very hot before it was frozen inside the comet. How this happened is still a mystery.

Future Exploration

Scientists still have a lot of questions about asteroids and comets. They want to learn why some asteroids like Vesta have iron cores while others do not. Does Ceres have an ocean? Scientists also want to understand how material in comets could have once been so hot.

To help answer these questions scientists have big plans for the future. They have already launched the *Dawn* space probe to study Vesta and Ceres. *Dawn* will orbit Vesta in 2011. Cameras on *Dawn* will take pictures of the rock inside Vesta's giant crater. Then *Dawn* will move on to Ceres in 2015. That's when scientists hope to find out if Ceres has an ocean of water.

The *New Horizons* space probe is on its way to study trans-Neptunian objects. It will fly past the dwarf planet Pluto in 2015. *New Horizons* will send back the first close-up images of Pluto.

A space probe named *Rosetta* is on its way to orbit a comet and land on its surface. *Rosetta* will reach the comet in 2014. *Rosetta* will drop a lander robot to the comet's surface to drill into the nucleus. Scientists can then use microscopes on the lander to study the nucleus.

Future exploration could answer many questions about our solar system. Studying space rocks and comets might even hold answers about how our solar system formed billions of years ago.

artist illustration of *Rosetta* on a comet

Glossary

atmosphere (AT-muh-sfeer)—the layer of gases that surrounds some dwarf planets, moons, planets, and stars

atom (A-tuhm)—an element in its smallest form

crater (KRAY-tuhr)—a hole made when large pieces of rock crash into the surface of an asteroid, dwarf planet, moon, or planet

friction (FRIK-shuhn)—the force created by a moving object as it rubs against something else

gravity (GRAV-uh-tee)—a force that pulls objects together; gravity increases as the mass of objects increases or as objects get closer

molecular cloud (muh-LEK-yuh-lur KLOUD)—a cloud trillions of miles across made mostly of hydrogen atoms bound together; new stars form deep within the cores of molecular clouds

nucleus (NOO-klee-uhss)—the lump of ice, snow, rock, and dust that moves around the Sun; a nucleus forms into a comet when it is warmed by the Sun

orbit (OR-bit)—the path an object follows as it goes around an asteroid, dwarf planet, planet, or star

solar wind (SOH-lur WIND)—particles blowing away from the Sun at 250 to 500 miles (400 to 800 km) per second

Read More

Prinja, Raman K. *Comets, Asteroids, and Meteors.* Universe. Chicago: Heinemann Library, 2008.

Sherman, Josepha. *Asteroids, Meteors, and Comets.* Space! New York: Marshall Cavendish Benchmark, 2010.

Sparrow, Giles. *Destination Asteroids, Comets, and Meteors.* Destination Solar System. New York: PowerKids Press, 2010.

Internet Sites

FactHound offers a safe, fun way to find Internet sites related to this book. All of the sites on FactHound have been researched by our staff.

Here's all you do:

Visit *www.facthound.com*

Type in this code: 9781429664943

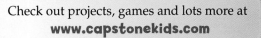

Super-cool stuff!

Check out projects, games and lots more at
www.capstonekids.com

Index